Change Your Attitude

Change Your Life

Insight Publishing Company
Sevierville, Tennessee

Published by Insight Publishing Company
P.O. Box 4189
Sevierville, Tennessee 37864

Printed in the United States of America
Cover Design: Russ Hollingsworth

ISBN 1-885640-89-7

In Loving Memory

My daddy Murry Brown Sr. for showing me the true meaning of "Love Thy Neighbor."

My mama Lucille Brown for her laughter, her love and her prayers.

My brother Murry Brown Jr. for setting a perfect example on the importance of having and becoming "true" friends.

My sister Nicey J. Brown for her smile, her determination and her willingness to help others.

My "Nanny" Thelma Brown Sanders for always greeting me with a smile.

Rev. M.E. Williams for his constant words of encouragement.

Dedication

To my wife Barbara: I have never loved another woman as much as I love you! Thanks for believing in my belief.

To our daughters Destiny and Britany: What can I say? You two have been a direct blessing from God. I am very proud of the both of you and thanks for helping me enjoy "fatherhood." Peace out!

v

Acknowledgments

To my sisters Thelma and Brenda: Thanks for setting such a great example for me to follow. May God continue to bless you...to bless others!

To my niece Natesha: You have proven how through faith, you can overcome adversity. Your mom is very proud of you.

To Les Brown: Thanks for helping me realize, "It's Possible."

Many thanks to Willie Jolley, Keith Harrell, Susan Taylor, Jim Rohn, Zig Ziglar, Dr. and Mrs. Joe Samuel Ratliff and the entire Brentwood Baptist Church family, The Southern University System, Nadia Graves, Barbara Thompson, David Wright and his excellent staff at Insight Publishing, Leigh Skinner, Brenda Keefer and Russ Hollingsworth, Jackie Preston, Dr. James Ward, "Main Street", Malcolm Brown, the "fellas," and a host of relatives and friends who have always believed in me!

And most of all, to the Creator of the Universe: All I can say is "How Great Thou Art."

"Live out of your imagination instead of your memory."

-Les Brown
American author and motivator

Foreword
by Les Brown

There's an old saying in which I believe strongly: If you're going to tell people how to win in life, "be the message that you bring." Dennis S. Brown is one of the most powerful speakers on the circuit today. But more than that, he is a person of integrity, perseverance and class. At a very low and difficult period in my life, a friend said to me, "Things are not going to get better for you until you change your attitude." At first I did not believe him, but I later found out he was right. If you want to experience more happiness, improve your health or earn more money--whatever your heart's desire-- "Change Your Attitude-Change Your Life" will show you how. Every day life demands of us -*"Show me what you're working with."* And if you don't have the right attitude, you will be defeated by the difficulties, tragedies and challenges that life constantly throws at us. This life-altering book will teach you how to roll with the punches of life and asks, *"Is this all you've got?"*

Dennis S. Brown proves life might knock you down, but you don't have to stay there. He says you are more powerful than you think.

You can't always control what happens to you. However, you can always choose the kind of attitude you embrace in response to what happens.

It is your birthright to be happy, healthy and prosperous. As you read this book, you will begin to unlock the hidden treasures of your unhappy potential and release your personal power to master your destiny and live the life others only dream about. Once you work with and apply these attitude-changing methods, and when it becomes second nature to you, your life will never be the same again. When you change your attitude, you don't just *go* through things, you *grow* through them and become stronger and more enlightened.

You are about to discover what the top achievers do to keep the right attitude when times get tough, and you don't feel like getting out of bed. It happens to the best of us. In my battle with prostate cancer, Dennis' attitude and words kept me going, and I believe he can do the same for you.

Dennis S, you've done me proud.
This has been Mrs. Mamie Brown's Baby Boy, ***Les Brown***.

Contents

"Attitude: The good news is, you don't have to buy it, but you do have to develop it!"

-Keith D. Harrell
American author and motivator

Chapter one

THE TIME IS NOW TO CHANGE YOUR ATTITUDE

The words I have written in this book may not bring you to your feet, but I can only hope that the information and inspiration of my words will bring you to your senses. The things I have written about may not sound good, but they will definitely be words that are good and sound. Since I can not teach you what I do not know and I would not lead you where I

1

would not go, I do want you to do one thing over and over again as you read this book, repeat the phrase: "The only difference between a good day & a bad day is your Attitude."™

Many times during one of my motivational speeches, participants will lean back in their chairs as if to say to me, "Motivate me! I didn't want to be here in the first place!" That's okay! I could not have motivated them if I had tried. Motivation is and has always been an inside job. You must be able to motivate yourself. If you do not think motivation is important, consider the following situations: Is it possible that you can lose all of your tangible possessions? You can lose your home through financial ruin or natural disasters. Circumstances can cause you to lose your automobile or any of your material possessions. Your attitude, however, is locked up inside you and may only be lost when *you* decide to let it go!

Developing a positive attitude may or may not be easy for you.

If you want to develop a good attitude, you have to like yourself a lot. In fact, many would argue that you have to love yourself. Can you imagine waking up in the morning, walking to the mirror and exclaiming, "Hey, you're all right! Imagine the power of affirming yourself every morning. You have to talk to yourself in the mirror every day. Some days will be more difficult than others. Unfortunately, there will be some days when you look in the mirror and say, "Hey, you're okay without much enthusiasm and that's okay, as long as it's just once in a while.

Life is too short to be miserable. Your goal must be to wake up every morning with enthusiasm! Approach each new day with positive expectancy. Try believing that each day comes with its own set of problems and solutions and that you will do your best to be a part of the solutions, not the problems. You must look in that mirror every morning and repeat, "I'm all right! Perhaps your family will think you have lost your mind, but that's okay.

Your dog may even think you're a little nuts, but that's okay, too. Remember, many people before you have proved beyond a shadow of a doubt that if you keep telling yourself that you are all right, you will start to believe that you are all right. If you start believing it, you will start acting that way and if you start acting that way, other people will believe it and change the way they have been treating you.

All of us know positive, self-assured people who walk into a room and light it up with their presence. They walk into a room and people say, "It is so good to see you! These people literally light up the room on their way in. On the other hand, there are others who light up a room on their way out! Trust me--you do not want to light up a room on your way out! Most of the time, the difference between these two types of people is their attitude and the things they believe to be true about themselves. Could it be possible that the people who light up the room when they enter truly believe that "The only difference between a good day

4

& a bad day is your Attitude? ™

Agreeing that it is great to be affirmed, nothing feels better than someone letting us know that there is something they like about us. However, affirmations do not necessarily have to come from others. We can use affirmations as a tool and affirm ourselves. One such affirmation is *the time is now!* As I travel across the country giving motivational speeches and training sessions, I always ask my audiences, "What time is it? Most of the time they will shout out the time of day or night. I then instruct them to say, *"the time is now!"* Then, during my presentation, every time I ask what time is it, the audience joins together in a chorus of *"the time is now!* Every time the audience repeats this affirming phrase, they seem to get louder. I have seen participants from my presentations in elevators, bathrooms, and halls after my programs and many of them smile at me and say, *"the time is now"* and, "The only difference between a good day and a bad day is my attitude. I hope you caught the difference between the affirmation I gave and the affirmation the participants received. If not, here it is. I said, "The only difference between a good day & a bad day is *your* Attitude. ™ They remembered it as *my* attitude.

Remember, "The only difference between a good day & a bad day is your Attitude! ™ Hopefully, you will repeat the affirmation *the time is now!*-throughout this book because I want you to go out into the world and set in motion what you have learned within these pages. I can write as dynamically as I can, speak as eloquently as I can and even plead with you as sincerely as I can. However, only you can decide to change your attitude and go out and activate the principles you learn in this book while you still have a chance!

Some years ago, I read a thought-provoking quote that helped change my life forever. The quote read, "He who angers you, conquers you. I don't know about you but I don't like being conquered! All of us have heard people say, "So-and-so person made me mad! Well, no one *made* you do anything; you decided to get mad. You let someone else "rent space in your head and control your emotions. In other words, someone conquered you! Perhaps if the person had developed "The only difference between a good day & a bad day is your attitude ^{TM} mentality, he or she may have thought, "I can't change another person's behavior. I can only change how I respond to it! This attitude would have insured a positive rather than a negative result. Also, before we respond to someone in a negative tone, we need to ask ourselves, "Could this wait?

"Whenever you journey within...you will never be without."

-Zen Proverb

Chapter two

THE MAGNIFICENT MOVIE: A VISION

To get the most out of life and enjoy the abundance that you were created to enjoy, you need to have a vision. You may have a vision that is not as clear as you would like it to be. That's okay. Development is the key to almost everything. So, you must work to develop a clear vision. You need to *see* yourself in the winner's circle! You need to feel the joy of winning and hear the applause of the crowd in your mind's eye.

9

It can be compared to going to the movies and seeing clips of the coming attractions. When I graduated from college, one of my goals was to be self-employed. I simply wanted to accomplish more in a shorter period of time and I knew that working for someone else would hold me back. Then, the questions started. What was I going to do and how was I going to do it? I didn't have the slightest idea, but I just kept telling myself that I was all right with my vision. I went to work as an accountant for a CPA firm, got married and in time, we had our first daughter and a few years later, we had our second daughter. It was during this time that the entrepreneur feeling started to hit me really hard, and my vision kept haunting me. My dreams of working for myself were consuming a large percentage of my thoughts. I started diligently thinking and praying about it. By the time we had our second daughter, I decided I would go home and tell my wife that I was going to quit my job, work for myself and become a nationally-known motivational speaker. As I think about it now, it was at that very moment that I had to put up or shut up about this thing called positive attitude! I went home and told my wife I was quitting my salaried, comfortable, steady job. She looked at me and paused for what seemed like an eternity and then she said to me, "Hey! Are you crazy? I said, "No! I am not crazy. You see, the only way I am going to find out whether I am going to be a success or a failure is to try! I owe it to you and I owe it to our daughters, Destiny and Britany and I owe it to myself! I left her with my confidence, my smile and what has become known as the husband's famous line, "You are just going to have to trust me on this one! To say that she reluctantly agreed would be an understatement, but agree she did, and I went out on the motivational speaking circuit. Perhaps you already know what it takes to be a motivational speaker. Suffice it to say, the key to becoming a professional motivational speaker is exposure! You must have people around to hear that you are a motivational speaker. I would go to bus stops and say, "I have a speech. Would you like to hear it? They would say, "No, get out of the way! But, as fate would

11

have it, at that time, I was the chairman of the deacon board at Brentwood Baptist Church in Houston, Texas. Brentwood Baptist Church has between 10,000 to 12,000 members, depending on which day you speak to the pastor! One of my duties was to assign speakers every month (are you getting ahead of me?). Since I needed exposure and I was the person charged with the responsibility of assigning speakers, guess who was the featured speaker in many instances?

As I look back, it has been a great privilege speaking at my own church. Not only do I know and love the people there, I have gotten a lot of help and referrals from Brentwood and I am still a faithful member. Please believe me when I tell you that I am a guy who is living his dream. I wake up every morning excited about what may happen that day. I go to bed every night excited and grateful because I feel that God has been good to me by giving me a mind that can entertain visions and dream dreams about the future!

At this point it would be foolish of me to suggest that there were no sacrifices that have to be made to get what you want. In my opinion, one of the most intelligent questions you must ask yourself is, "How badly do I want to accomplish my vision? When I decided to be a public speaker, I went from being an accountant to throwing newspapers from 4 a.m. to 6 a.m. to supplement my income in order to provide for my family. I don't know about you, but for me 4 a.m. to 6 a.m. is prime sleeping time! I had to make that sacrifice, but it was something I really wanted to do. I was a happy paper thrower! The first week, I gave all my papers away because I thought I couldn't have any newspapers left over. However, my manager told me that the next time, I was only supposed to throw them to the addresses on my route. But, that was okay with me because I was operating under the principle of *the time is now*! Regardless of my lost sleep and mistakes, I knew that "The only difference between a good day & a bad day is your Attitude. ™

We all know there are radar detectors in airports. What would happen if they put an attitude detector over the door of your house and you couldn't get in the door with a bad attitude? How many of you would have to change addresses? *The time is now* to understand that your attitude is everything! Recent studies show that your attitude and personality will get you much farther than any other characteristic you possess! Your attitude is even more important than your technical skills. If people like you, they will go out of their way to help you. However, you must first like yourself. Some people wake up angry! How can anyone wake up angry? Everyone should be thankful every morning to wake up-period! Life is too short for negative attitudes.

"Most people will go out of their way for you, if they just simply like you."

-Dennis S. Brown

"Hey!

You're alright!"

-Dennis S. Brown

Chapter three

WITH WHOM DO YOU ASSOCIATE?

I don't know about you, but I like being happy! It didn't take me too many years to figure out that, generally speaking, birds of a feather *do* flock together. People migrate to like-minded people most of the time. Athletes hang out with other athletes, attorneys hangout with other attorneys and so on. It didn't take me long to figure out that if I wanted to be happy, I would have to hang out with happy people. Conversely, if you

17

want to be sad, hang out with sad people. If you want to be negative-need I say more? It is a simple formula and the question you must ask yourself is, "Are you hanging out with the right people? "Who are you associating with? It has been postulated that in no small measure, your success or your failure will be based on two things-the books you read or the information you take in and the people with whom you associate with. The questions then become, "Am I reading the right books? Am I associating with the right people? It might interest you to know that in America, which is one of the richest countries on the face of the earth, the percentage of Americans who own library cards is about three percent! The average number of books that adults buy per year is one! The most astonishing fact that I have read is that 57 percent of Americans have never read a book from cover-to-cover. Even more disturbing is the statement that out of all the millions of books published each year in the United States, only 10 percent are read through the second chapter! In my opinion, if you want to become a leader, simply become a reader! It is a simple process. All readers may not be leaders, but I'm sure most, if not all leaders, are readers.

If you want to change your life, you must start reading! I have never been to a library where there is a sign flashing, "Sorry, we are all out of books today! It is just not like that! You need to read as much as you can. My challenge to you is to take a hard, honest look at yourself to determine whether or not you are on the right track as far as your education is concerned. Do you read? Do you attend seminars or workshops? If you can't find time to read, most great books are on audio cassette tapes. I listen to tapes in my car all the time. I call it my "Auto University. Believe me, your education from this point on is up to you, Remember, *the time is now!* Life is too short for any other affirmation. I don't want you to wake up one day and find that you are "dead, just to realize you didn't enjoy yourself while you were living! You must enjoy life now-while you are able.

Your life would be better if you were to wake each morning with the enthusiasm necessary to seek out people who could help you become better with a desire to cultivate a positive attitude. It is very important that you have self-confidence and pass it on to people around you! This is very important.

Our youngest daughter, Britany, at the age of four said, "Daddy, when I am five, would you please take the training wheels off my bike because I will be a big girl?   I said, "Okay, we will do that!   Some time after that, she said, "Today's my birthday!   So, our oldest daughter, Destiny and I went out and took the training wheels off her bike. We dressed Britany up like a football player, complete with a helmet and pads, because we knew she would be falling off her bike until she learned how to ride on two wheels. After a few tumbles on the concrete, Britany took off by herself and I yelled, "Britany, you are doing great!   She turned her little head toward me and said, "Daddy, attitude is everything! I told my neighbor, "That's my child!

My point is that you must pass your positive attitude on to others if you want to live in a better world. You simply *must* pass it on. Try asking yourself this question: "Do your children run *to* you or *from* you when you go home? If they are running away from you, maybe you need a slight attitude adjustment. You need to have fun with your children while you still have a chance! My wife Barbara says that she has three children-the two girls and me! That's okay because I like to have fun! Sometimes when I arrive home from a speaking engagement, our daughters will jump up and down and shout, "Daddy's home! Daddy's home! Then I jokingly tell my wife that she should also jump up and down when I arrive home. Her reply was simply, "You must have been dreaming and you just woke up! *That's okay-dream anyway!*

"*When you tell the truth, you don't have to remember what you've said.*"

-Dennis S. Brown

Chapter four

IF THERE'S SMOKE, IS THERE FIRE?

It is important that you understand that things are not always as bad as they appear. My wife called me one day in January after we had just moved into our new home. She said, "Dennis, every time I turn the dryer on, the fuse box starts smoking." Worried that it might cause damage-not to mention how dangerous it could be-I told her to turn the dryer off and I assured her I was on my way home. I thought to myself, "I'm not mechanically inclined, but I will act like I am when I get home. I walked in the door and said, "Hey, what's wrong?" She said, "I told you! Every time I turn on the dryer, the fuse box starts smoking!" She turned the dryer on and I looked outside and smoke was everywhere. I told her to turn it off. I went outside to investigate, but I didn't see anything burned or any smoke so I did what any loving and intelligent husband would have done. I called for help! A young man came and asked me what the problem was so I boldly told him that my wife said, "When the dryer is turned on, the fuse box starts smoking!" He told me to turn the dryer on and he would check to see what was wrong. I turned the dryer on and he went outside to check. When he came in he said, "Mr. Brown, I have discovered your problem. When the hot air from your dryer meets the cold air from outside, that is called steam! Mr. Brown, that will be $35." *Remember this very important point: In life, you will deal with a lot of people, so every time someone blows smoke in your face it does not necessarily mean there is fire behind it.*

It is simply a part of living for people to go through the many challenges in their lives. Often the first person they meet during one of these major challenges just happens to be you! But, you only know part of the story! Sometimes we want to strike back without realizing that people are just ventilating and we need to step back and let them do it. People in the entire counseling industry make their living listening to people who have problems. Perhaps if each of us listened to other people's problems and respected the fact that they are going through difficult changes, they would not have to spend so much money on counseling. When we are honest with ourselves, we must admit that we have days that we need to blow off steam as well! Try to think of the last time that you erupted and blew off steam. Was there someone there listening to you or trying to understand your point of view? Probably not. We tend not to lose our temper with people who we perceive to be on our side. We need to remember, that *the time is now* to be sensitive to the hurts and problems of others so that we may enjoy life as much as we can while our clock is still ticking.

In Stephen Covey's book, "The Seven Habits of Highly Effective People , he tells the story of being on the subway while every thing around him was calm and tranquil. Before long, a young man came on board with his kids. To say they were making a lot of noise would be an understatement. Covey thought to himself that if the man did not tell his kids that they were making too much noise, then he will have to tell them in no uncertain terms. Well, the kids got louder and louder so Covey slammed down his newspaper and said, "Sir, do you realize that your kids are making too much noise? You need to do something about it. The young man lifted his head and said, "Sir, we just left the hospital and my wife, the children's mother just died of cancer. I don't know how to handle it and I am afraid they don't either. I am sorry!

Covey then shifted his attitude from angry to concern because he only knew part of the story. How often do we fly off the handle when we only know part of the story? To be happy and reach your dreams, you have to show some compassion when confronted with people who are acting erratically or different from you! You must learn to love people in the circumstances where you meet them. Also, you must love yourself because, if you fill your heart with enough love, there will not be enough room for hate! If you keep filling your heart with love and expect good things to happen to you, you can truly say, "Hey, I am all right! And, it will be obvious to everyone who meets you.

"One kind word can warm three winter months."

-Japanese Proverb

Chapter five

MAKE CONVERTS FOR GOOD

Drug dealers recruit! Pimps recruit! Gangs recruit! Bad folks have no problem trying to recruit other bad or weak people to join their causes. So, we need to try to recruit all people, strong or weak, to our side and not be a part of their negative way of looking at things. Many times, especially at work, you meet people and say, "Hi, how are you doing? Sometimes they will say, "Well, I'm hanging! I am waiting on five o'clock!   When they ask you how you are doing say, "Hey, I'm doing great! I'm working on a great project! They might look at you strangely, but that is okay, too. Remember, we are trying to recruit them to a more positive way of thinking because we know that their lives and our lives will be better if we succeed. And, because we do not have control over time and circumstance in many areas, the present may be the only opportunity we will ever have. Remember, in the destruction of the World Trade Center on September 11, 2001, thousands of people just like you and I died in a horrific attack. In the aftermath of this tragedy, there were countless stories of good, positive, caring people helping each other to safety. The point is this: Helping people to be positive rather than negative will increase your enjoyment in life. In addition, their positive attitude will shine as a light for others. They will be a beacon in the negative sea of darkness for those who are in trouble and need a change of attitude and spirit. Remember that attitude is everything! We all must remember that! Because we're all in this thing together!

Some people do not like to talk about death, but I am not one of those people. The fact is, we are all going to die! What is not a fact is whether or not we are going to enjoy living! That's where attitude plays the most important role. You need to decide right now that today is the first day of the rest of your life. You need to start making your life more fun! Contrary to popular belief, you can have fun and still be productive. You can be more productive than you have ever imagined if you put yourself in balance and in check. Putting yourself in balance means to lighten up a little. It means that you don't take things and especially yourself so seriously. Putting yourself in check means to think before you speak and don't make judgements until you have at least tried to hear the whole story. It is never too late to have a good attitude. Your attitude is not hereditary so please do not say, "My mama was mean or my daddy was mean, so it is in my genes! You need to change your "mental genes because you need to enjoy life while you have a chance! Changing to a

31

positive attitude is critical. You need to learn how to laugh and smile as often as you can! Even if you have to *laugh and smile on credit*! Each morning, when you are looking in the mirror while combing your hair and getting ready to begin a new day, practice your smile. Down through the years, thousands of speakers, trainers, authors and philosophers have affirmed the positive effects of smiling. People who train others how to develop a telephone personality actually say that everyone can "see a smile over the telephone lines. We don't smile because we don't think it's important or we don't remember how effective it is. Believe me, *the time is now* to smile. It is not only important; it is life changing.

When you are in front of the public, a smile is very important! You must practice it because what people notice first are your facial expressions. Even if you are using a smile as a tool for your own improvement, you should still smile. Even if you don't particularly like somebody, it will still help you and them if you smile. Remember, a positive attitude is much better than a negative one, so enjoy life while you have the chance!

"Enjoy yourself. It's later than you think."

-Chinese Proverb

Chapter six

DO IT NOW!

I think Whittier said it best when he wrote, *"The clock of life is wound but once and no one has the power to tell just when the hand will stop, at late or early hour. I do today the urgent tasks. I do it with a will! I wait not for tomorrow for my hands may then be still!"* Don't put off what you can do today for later because later may never come! Stop putting off telling your kids how much you love and appreciate them. Tell them now while you still have the opportunity. Call that special friend that you haven't called in three or four years. You know, the one you have been telling yourself you were going to call. Sometimes, when someone we know dies, we think, "Boy, if I had only said or done... By then, it is too late! Simply do it now!

Some people take pride in being sarcastic and cruel to others. Their attitude might be, "I don't care what anyone says. I was mean when I woke up this morning and I will be mean when I go to sleep! If that is the way you feel, I'm afraid you are going to have a hard time with this book based on positive lifestyles. I can attest to the fact that if you want to bring or attract more people to you and you want to bring more joy and excitement to your life, you must remember that "The only difference between a good day & a bad day is your Attitude! ™

If you don't think a positive attitude is a valuable asset in every aspect of life, consider that all research in the past few decades leads to the conclusion that laughter is really the best medicine. Volumes have been written about humor as a healing device. Laughter releases chemicals in our bodies that actually heal. Evidence and personal testimony lead us to believe that humor and laughter have cured cancer as well as other serious, life-threatening illnesses in many patients. If you are to be happy and content with yourself, you must have joy in your life. You see, when it comes to true joy, you have to learn how to laugh most of the time! When was the last time you had a really gut-wrenching belly laugh and said, "Whoo, I haven't laughed like that in a long time? Don't make it so long! Find things to laugh about because laughter is healthy. Have you ever noticed how happy people are healthy people? Do you see the correlation? Once again, you have to enjoy life while you have the opportunity. Remember, your life's clock keeps ticking.

"A setback is a setup for a comeback."

-Willie Jolley
American author and motivator

Chapter seven

PREPARE YOURSELF FOR BATTLE

Not too long ago, sportswriters were interviewing Evander Holyfield, then the heavyweight boxing champion of the world. The interview took place just before his last fight with Mike Tyson. Some writer made the comment, "Evander, you are about to climb into the ring with Mike Tyson one more time. You beat this guy the last time but this is powerful Mike Tyson we are talking about. He is going to be really angry with you this time! The writer's words were prophetic. Little did he know just how angry Tyson was going to be! The writer's question continued, "Aren't you afraid of getting hit by such a powerful force? Without any hesitation, Holyfield said, "No! I am not afraid! When the day comes that I am afraid of getting hit by another boxer will be the time the licks will hurt the most! Holyfield prepared himself both mentally and physically for the battle and, having prepared himself to the best of his ability, he was not afraid of anything or anybody. Here is a great question. What battles are you preparing yourself for? Or, are you simply sitting back, unprepared, and letting life pass you by? Many people live their lives on the "Thank God it's Friday principle. They are content to rush through their life from Monday morning at eight o'clock through Friday evening at five o'clock. Their life begins at five o'clock on Friday and ends at eight o'clock on Monday morning. In more vivid terms, these people live only 38 percent of their life and virtually squander the other 62 percent. For example, if they live to be 75 years of age before dying, they only have truly lived twenty-eight and a half years. How do you measure up on this scale? Are you living a fulfilling life? Are you walking around with a sign that reads, *"Here lies John Smith who died at 28 and will be buried at 75?"*

Sometimes life is hard, and, we have heard that life is not a dress rehearsal. *The time is now!* Live now-in the present. Make every day the best you can and you will never have to apologize to yourself or anyone else about your actions. Remember, practice may not make you perfect, but it will make you better, so we have to prepare for life as if it were the most important thing that we will ever do. Because, it will be!

For me, it is simpler and more effective to set aside a certain time to do certain things, especially when it comes to planning and introspection. I find that the best time to talk to my kids is just before they go to sleep. That's when I tell them how much I love and care for them. At that time I can get their attention.

41

Most of the time they are quiet and receptive. Given the option, I would rather tell them I love them when they are more likely to listen and think about what I say rather than trying to tell them I love them while they are playing or watching television. Also, nighttime is the best time for me to talk to myself. This is the time I ask myself this question, "What did I do today to get closer to my goal? I must admit, sometimes the answer is, "Nothing. If you have hopes, dreams and goals and keep saying "nothing to the same question, I guarantee you that you are not going to realize your goals. You must work on your goals daily. It's like eating an elephant. You must take one bite at a time. I know it's trite, however, it's also true that a journey of a thousand miles begins with a single step.

My advice to you is to learn to tackle things while you have the opportunity and to hang out with people who will help you get where you want and need to be. A simple caution: You have to watch and be careful with whom you share your dreams.

Unfortunately, everybody is not going to be jumping up and down for the opportunity to insure your success. Sometimes, you shouldn't tell what street your parade is going down so people who really don't want you to succeed won't rain on it!

First, you must be excited about yourself and your prospects of future successes! What does this have to do with attitude? Everything! You must learn to get into the habit of expecting good things to happen to you! Positive expectancy is not just a phrase. It has changed thousands of lives for the better. It is not a "feel good philosophy; positive expectancy is a tool you can use to shape your future. Your only other option is to be fearful and have thoughts of failure. These thoughts take the form of, "I can't do it. or " I don't have the education necessary. or "No one in my family has ever done it before. " Consider NBA star Avery Johnson-all five feet and eleven inches of him. He went from team to team and was even released from one team on Christmas Eve! Yet he went on to become a starting point guard for the NBA San Antonio Spurs and eventually hit the winning

43

shot to propel the Spurs to become NBA Champions in 1999 because he still had enough faith in himself and his abilities. As he, and many others have proven, you can do anything you set your mind to. If you can believe that, trust me, you will go a long way in life! You *can* do it! Every now and then, you must stretch yourself to simply see how far you can really go. If there was a key to "making it" in life, my advice is: Prepare, prepare, prepare. Then, expect great results!

"Worry and faith are just like oil and water-they don't mix!

-Dennis S. Brown

"Think before you act."

-Dennis S. Brown

Chapter eight

WHAT DOES FAITH HAVE TO DO WITH ANYTHING?

One day, I went to pick up our daughter Britany from kindergarten and to my surprise, the teachers had my child in time-out! Imagine-my offspring in trouble! I said, "Brit, why are you in time-out today?   since it was not the first time. She said, "Daddy, they had us walking in this circle and I decided to walk out of the circle just to see what it was like. Trying not to look too pleased, inside I was saying to myself, "Now, that's *my* girl!   Looking at the situation from the teacher's point of view and trying to be the most helpful father I could be, I told her she must follow the rules set out by the school. Having said that, I really believe that sometimes all of us must walk out of the circles in our lives. Sometimes we simply have to step outside our usual way of doing things and exercise our faith so we will grow and learn from the new experience. Having faith is one thing, but applying faith is a whole different ball game. Have you applied your faith lately? What have you done to move out of your comfort zone? What faith steps have you taken to insure your continued knowledge and growth? You might try believing, through faith, that sometimes you need to expect good things to happen and they do. I believe that many times, to your amazement, good things will happen. Exercising true faith or true belief means that you can crystalize a goal or an incident and actually feel it, see it, taste it and smell it each and every day as if it had already come to pass!

If you control your future with acts of faith, love has to play an integral role. You must show love to other people. On that note, let me give you my 30-second dissertation on cultural diversity. If a baby is born in Africa, China or in your hometown, a baby's cry is a baby's cry. Laughter is laughter. A hurt heart is a hurt heart and happiness is happiness! Are we diverse? Of course we are. We can look at each other, interact with each other and understand the differences. What I find so incredible, however, is that too often we do not understand that we are also all alike. In every society in the world, people of all ages, races, and creeds want to be loved, appreciated, hugged and told they are someone special. Do you need a hug today to affirm your specialness? If you do, that is okay. Just find somebody you care about and hug them. Believe they will hug you back! You simply have to show sincere emotion and, if you are a male reading this, it is okay to show some emotion. Remember-you must do the things in life you have to do to make yourself feel "special while you still have the chance.

Will pressures come into your life? Absolutely! Life is full of pressures. Fortunately for you, it is not what happens to you, it is how you react to what happens to you that will make a difference in your life! Stuff happens! When it happens, you have to understand that you have a choice. You can react any way you choose. If someone offends you, you can strike back with a vengeance or you can forgive that person. The choice is yours. So, you may say, "What does it have to do with attitude? Everything! *Remember-the time is now*! You have to learn to act and react on your inner beliefs. Act immediately on the principles that you have already decided upon. The choice is fight or forgive. But is that really a choice? Fighting hurts all parties. Forgiveness helps the forgiver. For example, if two people are estranged for several years because one person abused the other, is it not the one who was abused that is helped by simply forgiving the other person? The one guilty of abusing the other may not even know he or she has been forgiven. So, *the time is now* to begin making decisions on sound principles.

Making choices is much like eating an ice cream cone and watching the top half drop to the ground in a pile of dirt.

Assuming you don't pick it up and put it back on, you have a choice to make! You can either stand back and mourn what you have lost or you can enjoy what is left. If you are dealing with divorce, enjoy what you have left. If somebody in your family dies, enjoy what you have left. If you get passed over for a promotion on your job, beat them up! No, I'm just kidding! You have to enjoy what you have left! Attitude is everything! I can't express that to you strongly enough because you have to enjoy life while you have the chance!

"Therefore do not worry about tomorrow, for tomorrow will worry about itself. Each day has enough trouble of its own."

-Matthew 6:34

Chapter nine

LIGHTEN UP A LITTLE

One of America's most famous composers, Irving Berlin, who wrote "White Christmas, also wrote, "Count Your Blessings." In the song we are advised that "When you're worried and you can't sleep, just count your blessings instead of sheep, and you'll fall asleep counting your blessings. Many of us have a tendency to moan and groan about what we *don't* have, when in fact, we should enjoy what we *do* have. It's even easier to be negative when someone else is helping us moan and groan. Don't let someone else's "outside ruin your "inside.

When I go home at night, I go into my children's bedroom and see them in their rooms sound asleep. Quietly, I think, "How lucky can I be? Just look at these extraordinarily beautiful girls lying there looking just like their father! It gives me an opportunity to infuse humor into my life and insures that even if I have had a rotten day, I will not participate in a "pity party. You know the feeling. *The nobody-loves-me-but-me* and *I-am-in this-thing-all-by-myself* kind of party! I challenge you! The next time you start to have a pity party, go visit the nearest hospital or convalescent home. You don't have to say anything to anybody! If you can walk out of there still having a pity party, you have my sympathy! Simply having your health and wellness is a blessing to cherish. I had no idea how important good health was until I had minor surgery on my foot, (would you believe an old football injury?). I wore a little blue shoe and found that there was pain involved in simply putting one foot in front of the

54

other. Before, steps came automatically without any conscious effort on my part. But for a while after the surgery, I found that walking wasn't quite as easy as it used to be.

Not only do you need to stay away from pity parties, you need to learn how to take mini-vacations. When was the last time you sat back and watched a sunset or a sunrise, sat out at night and gazed at the stars, or walked through the grass with your shoes off, or rode in your car with the radio off? We could all learn a lot about living joyous lives from children because they have an energy and a faith that are unparalleled. Kids look at their parents and think, "I know my parents are going to take care of me. I know my parents will love me and protect me no matter what happens. Children have faith in their parents. They view them much like supreme beings. They have the faith to believe that they will be kept from harm. I wonder how different our lives would be if we never grew out of that phase and kept right on believing in our safeness. We should realize that we do have somebody to watch our backs. If you realize this, there is nothing that you cannot do! You would be more productive on your job, more happy and more creative.

People often ask others, "Why do you do what you do? Their reply might be, "Because I have been doing it that way for years. How can anyone live a joyous life filled with excitement if they keep on doing what they've always been doing and don't like it? My suggestion to you is simple-have fun doing what you are doing! Remember, when you die, your name will be on your tombstone and under your name will appear two dates. The first will be your date of birth. The second will be the date of your death. The most important thing on your tombstone, however, will be the *dash* between the two dates. The dash is important because that represents your life. On my tombstone, in addition to the usual stuff, it will read, "The only difference between a good day & a bad day is your Attitude! ™ (Now make sure it's on there, otherwise I may come back!). The question then becomes, what does that dash mean? What have you done? If something were to happen and you were to die today and the last line of your obituary read, "This person was known for... what would yours say? What have you done? Who have you helped? If you are not satisfied with that last line, begin today to change it because today really is the first day of the rest of your life! Perform some random acts of kindness toward others today. Remember, the law of reciprocity states that, "If you give, you will receive!

I say one simple prayer before I leave home each day: "God, please bless me to bless others. If I can do that, I know I will have a wonderful, spirit-filled day! If you go out and try to help people, give them compliments and make them laugh, it makes *you* feel better. Don't keep kindness, love and caring to yourself because life is too short for that. You have to go out and help as many people as you can. I know that some of you are probably thinking, "Mr. Brown, you don't understand. I have a horrible past! For me, the best way to illustrate how to handle the past is to take a look at the movie *The Lion King.* In the movie, Simba, the baby lion is complaining to the baboon about how his past is too painful and he doesn't want to go back and face it. The baboon says, "Just shut up! There are two things you can do about your past. You can either run from it or learn from it! Then, he slaps the lion on the head and Simba says, "Why did you do that?   The baboon says, "Don't worry about it; it's in the past! The baboon tried to hit him again but the lion ducked and the baboon said, "See, you learned from it! Our life is a lot like Simba's when it comes to our past. We can either *run* from it or we can *learn* from it. Believe me, if you decide to run, you are going to be running for the rest of your life!

"Everything is possible for him who believes."

-Mark 9:23

"The time is now!"

-Dennis S. Brown

Chapter ten

FAKE IT 'TIL YOU MAKE IT!

You need to make a stand and put your belief system on the line just as Evander Holyfield did in the example as shown previously in an earlier chapter in this book. Your beliefs are a result of your preparation, so the key question becomes: What are you preparing for and where do you see yourself? Some of us plan our vacations with more accuracy than we plan our lives. When we are planning for our vacations, we spend time requesting a hotel room with a certain view and check available sights that will fit the needs of everyone in our party. We may decide in advance where we will eat certain meals and pay the required deposits. We may call, write or e-mail for maps and tourist attractions and even get a customized road trip package. Since so many people have access to the Internet, we may even print out a road map that begins at our residence and ends at the exact address of our destination. Sadly, most people give very little consideration to planning when it comes to their lives. Worse still, many people have no idea where they are going in life and less understanding of where they've been.

Having a positive attitude will not necessarily cause you to do anything specific, but it will allow you to do almost everything you are doing even better! If you have a great, positive attitude, you will be a better parent, co-worker, brother, sister, student- well you get the picture! If your attitude is right, you are immune from the disease called "I'm. I'm this or I'm that!

Think of all the people you know as being a team. Is there an "I in team? No! Remember a team is only as strong as its weakest member. Therefore, each of us should try to help each other make our days a little bit better. Even if we are not yet at the point where we are positive most of the time, we just have to fake it 'til we make it!

I used to drive an older car that had perhaps seen its better days. When I drove my daughter Destiny to school, she would wait until we got two or three blocks away from the school and she would say, "Daddy you can let me out right here, because I want to walk with my friends. When I would look out the window, none of her friends would be in sight! So I would say to her, "No, if the car stops I will need you *and* your friends to help push it! But, that was okay because I knew that when I could afford it, I would buy a newer automobile for the family, one that would make everyone proud.

Shortly after beginning my speaking career, I would be booked at these nice five-star hotels. There are some cars you do not valet! I had one of them. I would park past the hotel and by the time I would reach the hotel, I would be perspiring and people would ask me what was wrong. One day I had a speaking engagement at The Houstonian, a place where you can't park a few blocks away and walk to the conference center. They force you to valet there. Let me paint a picture for you. I was in Houston, Texas in August and I had owned that car which had no air conditioning for many years. I drove up to the entrance gate, my window was already down, and the young man asked for my identification. I gave him my drivers license and upon review, he smiled and said, "Mr. Brown, they are expecting you so please pull up to the next building where they will valet your car. Now, I had to talk to myself. I said, "Okay, Dennis. You travel all over, telling people to have a positive attitude and to fake it 'til you make it! Now what are you going to do? I drove up to about a few feet from where they valet your cars and I rolled my windows up and acted like I had cool air! I was greeted by the attendant, stood tall and told him to have a great day! The whole time I was gone, the valet tried to work on my air conditioning. When I came back for my car at the lunch break, the valet said he tried to adjust the air, but couldn't get it to work. So I looked at him and said, "I'll just roll down the windows for now and I can take care of it later! You see, you just have to fake it 'til you make it! If you want a promotion, go into your supervisor's office and sit in his or her chair just to see how it feels. Remember one important thing-don't get caught! If you want to live in an upscale neighborhood, just go there and park and say to yourself that the house you see really belongs to you! Sure, the owners will probably ask you to leave, but that is okay. If you want a luxury automobile, go to a dealer and get into that car and smell the leather. Imagine yourself driving your family to an important event where you will see all your friends. I used to visit expensive clothing stores and talk to the suits! Imagine the looks I got when the salesperson saw me addressing a suit and saying, "Hey there, Papa is coming!" Don't let life get you down simply because you have not yet "made it." Life is too short; the *time is now* and "The only difference between a good day & a bad day is your Attitude."™

"*Tell people you love them while you have a chance!*"

-Lucille Brown

"My Mama

"Rent if you must.

Own if you can!"

-Murry Brown Sr.

"My Daddy"

Chapter eleven

REMEMBER, I LOVE YOU

I went to visit my mama a few years ago. She is more than my mama. She is my best friend. I used to call home just to hear her laugh. One thing my mama loved to do was talk on the phone. When call waiting came out we used to say, "Mama, please get call waiting! She would always say she didn't need it. We finally talked her into getting it and then when we called she was very comical. She would say, "One moment please.

Our mama had broken her ankle and my family and I went to visit. She was the same sweet, caring Mama she always was. I will always remember the way Mama ended her phone conversations with, "And always remember-I love you! How often do we hear those three words? How often do we say those three words? If you want to hear them more often, you need to say them more often! Tell people you love them while you have the chance!

One of my duties as a deacon of my church was to open the service with a prayer and a scripture. My mama called it "preaching. She asked me when I was "preaching again and I told her this Sunday. On the days I would "preach, I would mail Mama the tape of the service. She would play it for her friends so they could hear her boy "preach. On this Sunday, less than 12 hours after driving back to Houston, I received word that my mama had a heart attack and died! It was a major blow to me! Some days I miss my mama so much that it hurts.

But you know, I thank God for my mama. I thank God for my daddy. They didn't have a college degree or a high school diploma, but they had a Ph.D. in love and understanding! My parents taught us all a valuable lesson: *It is not what you leave for your children that makes a difference, it's what you leave in your children that's going to make the difference.* The question then becomes: What are you leaving in your children? Or more importantly, what are you leaving in yourself? If my mama was here today, she would tell you to listen to me. The key is you have to enjoy what you have while you have a chance! I carry a picture of my mama with me all the time, and I often wear my dad's cufflinks. Never forget where you came from or what your reason is to succeed!

I am sure you have friends that you can call on to make you feel better. Sometimes you must do that. The best definition I have ever heard of a friend is, "Someone who knows a lot about you, but likes you anyway! The question becomes: How many friends are calling on you to help them feel better? If your phone is not ringing, you need an attitude adjustment. Today is the first day of the rest of your life so try to help as many people as you can. When you are under pressure-and believe me, pressure will come-consider Pat Riley. When Riley was the coach of the Los Angeles Lakers, he wrote in his first book "Show Time," "What do you get when you squeeze an orange? Orange juice. What do you get when you squeeze a lemon? Lemon juice! What I am saying to you is that if you put enough pressure on people, what is inside has to come out! What are you filling yourself with on the inside? Have you noticed that some people handle pressure differently than others? The reason is that they are cushioning themselves with some good things on the inside. They have read some good books, listened to some positive tapes, hung out with positive people. You may need to ride around in your car with the radio off so you can get in touch with your emotions.

You have to learn how to smile even when you don't have anything to smile about. You do everything else on credit, so smile, even when you don't feel like it! What if I were to make you a proposition that every day I would give you $86,400 under the condition that you would have to invest that money wisely and if you did, I would write you a check every day for $86,400? What would you do? You would find ways to go out and invest it wouldn't you? Of course you would! Regardless of race, creed or color, we are all given 86,400 seconds every day. Your time is that valuable, so the question becomes, what are you doing with your time? Yesterday is a canceled check, tomorrow a promissory note and today it is cold, hard cash. You have to learn how to invest it wisely!

"If you love what you do, you'll never work a day in your life."

-Confucius

"The way to spell love with your children is T-I-M-E."

-Dennis S. Brown

"The only difference between a Good day & a Bad day is your Attitude!"™

-Dennis S. Brown

Chapter twelve

TURN YOUR WATER ON

If you want to ensure that you will receive positive input instead of negative input, you have to talk positively to yourself every day. Positive self-talk is critical. It's one of the few ways you can avoid other people telling you what you can and cannot do, think or achieve. Remember-thousands of people before you have, by their own example, proved that anything is possible. You must use the intelligence and imagination that

God gave you and that you, by your own decision, developed in order to actually visualize your goals and dreams. In other words, whatever your goal is, you must develop the ability to see it, smell it and tastes it as if it had already come to pass! It can happen. It has happened to me and it can happen to you. You just have to believe it!

Sound simple? It is simple, but not easy. You must commit yourself to develop a positive attitude in a mostly negative world. I remember going to a football game one beautiful Saturday afternoon where there were more than 100,000 people in attendance. As I was walking down the ramp, exiting the stadium after the game, I began to think that if I had left an article of clothing back at my seat, I would then have to go against the flow of the crowd. Imagine everyone walking in one direction getting out of the stadium and me, the only person in 100,000, going in the opposite direction! Get the picture? It may seem just as hard for you develop a positive attitude especially when everyone else is going in the opposite direction.

Change Your Attitude-Change Your Life

You might think that you are too old to change your attitude because you have been the way you are for years and years. If you only remember one thing from this book, remember this: *It is never too late to change.* If you really must test whether or not you're getting old there is only one test to take. *When you start having more regrets than you have dreams, you are getting old*! At this point, you must change! Many people have asked me, "What is the cutoff for dreams? There is none! Keep dreaming, planning and praying that good things as well as challenges will keep happening to you that will make you a better, more successful and happier person. Praying for inspiration instead of desperation is one of the keys. People like to be around happy people. Some people enjoy jumping on you and raining on your parade. At these times, it is doubly important to remain positive and hopeful about the decisions and the direction of your life. If you can do what is right regardless of the things other people say, think or do, eventually what is wrong will leave your life! Just stay positive and don't let negative people drag you down. Remember, negative people will drag you down only if you let them! You must keep your eyes straight ahead and never lose sight of your goal to remain committed, dedicated and excited about developing a positive attitude.

If you're a parent or if you plan to have children, I would like to share the most important fact I have learned about being a successful dad: Children spell love T-I-M-E! You have to *show* them that you love them by spending time with them. If you think your kids are not listening, believe me, they are always listening and watching you. Just think of how powerful you can make your children by simply passing on the desire and the ability for them to develop their own positive attitude. Would it not be wonderful to overhear a conversation where your child is saying to one of his or her friends, "The only difference between a good day & a bad day is your Attitude? ™

My desire and my prayer is that you are already developing a positive attitude! I hope that you are more positive now that you have read this book. After all, my concern for your attitude is the only reason I wrote this book. If your attitude has improved, I guarantee that your life will be just a little bit sweeter! You will find that a lot more people will like and appreciate you than you ever knew existed.

All of us need to develop our positive attitude. We must give it top priority while we still have an opportunity. Remember-tomorrow is not promised. The only promise we have is now! Do it now and expect good things to happen to you. I expected good things to happen to me and good things did happen. If you expect good things to happen to you, good things will happen to you as well. You will literally become what you think about! What do you spend most of your time thinking about? If you think about it, you are going to achieve it. Poverty or prosperity? If you think about *it*, you are going to achieve *it*!

I would like to challenge you. But first, I would like to commend you for taking time out to make yourself better. I would also like to commend you for doing something most people simply do not do-read an entire book! I now challenge you to take yourself to the next level. Now that you are finished with this book, you should be feeling pretty good about yourself. However, you may also feel good by taking a nice long shower. I heard a story once where a man said, "I felt so good yesterday, I stood in the shower for an hour and if I feel that good today...I will *turn the water on!* The information I have shared with you in this book would place you in the shower. However, if you want to turn the water on in your life, you must start applying the principles you learned in this book! I want you to turn on the water so high that others around you can feel it, taste it and see it. *Then you could assist me to spread the word to others around the world that* "The only difference between a good day & a bad day is your Attitude! ^{TM}

Pass it on!

Change Your Attitude - Change Your Life

Products You Can Purchase from Dennis S. Brown

Change Your Attitude - Change Your Life (Book) $15.95 each
10-20 copies (10% discount) $14.35 each
over 20 copies (15% discount) $12.76 each

The Time Is Now to Improve Your Attitude (Video) $29.95 each

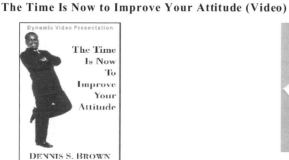

T- Shirt (The Most Popular Item!) Sz L, XL, XXL   **$12.00 each**
The Only Difference Between a Good Day & a Bad Day is Your Attitude!™

❏ Book _____ copies $ _____
❏ Video _____ copies $ _____
❏ T-Shirt _____ No. Units_____Size $ _____
Shipping & Handling _____ items X $1.50 $ _____
                                            TOTAL $ _____

Name_____
Address _____
City _____ St. _____ Zip _____
Check Number _____ Amount _____
MC / Visa _____ Exp. Date _____
Cardholder Signature _____

Send to: **Phone orders:**
Destiny Investments   1-800-634-5349
P.O. Box 740905
Houston TX 77274-0905

For additional information on
Products and Services of

Dennis S. Brown

Please call 1-800-634-5349

or visit us on the web at

www.dennissbrown.com